Visions & Glimpses

A short anthology by

Roger Lloyd Wood
1932 - 2001

RHU Christian Publications

Copyright © 2004 Sarah Wood

First Published 2004

All rights reserved.

No part of this publication may be reproduced or transmitted in any form or by any means, electronic or mechanical, including photocopy, recording or any information storage and retrieval system, without permission in writing from the publisher.

ISBN 0-9549273-0-3

Published by

RHU Christian Publications
The Vicarage,
Old Vicarage Close
Stithians,
Truro.
TR3 7DZ.

Preface

Born in a country Vicarage in 1932, my life has been varied and, for the most part, enjoyable because God has been there - and still is! Through wartime in a boarding school, banking, national service in the R.A.F. and home service with a missionary society; from a career in educational visual aids to redundancy, self-employment, a traffic warden, van driving and latterly, in Christian coffee shop ministry, counselling and pastoral work in the parish. In a marriage of over thirty years, the Lord has blessed us with two sons. Eight years ago I was diagnosed as having leukaemia, from which I believe the Lord is healing me. My wife and I are currently at theological college where she is training for the ministry, after which we shall return to Cornwall to exercise what we believe God has called us to - a joint ordained and lay ministry together in His Church.

I am not a theologian or an academic and it is rather in hindsight than in the present that I realise that God does speak to me. I have experienced fear and anxiety, joy and peace in my life, tempered with what I believe to be a simple but firm and growing faith that God is there and that He does care for me, for everyone, and meet us in our need when we seek Him out. Some of the things He has taught me and from which I have benefited, I have noted down and would like to share with others. This, then, is the purpose of this anthology.

Roger L. Wood (1993).

For our sons, Hadyn and Russell –
who were as determined as me to see their Dad's writing in print.

and

With many thanks to Martin Hogan for his patience, love and friendship as, with us and for us, he gathered material, collated, and produced this anthology to God's praise and glory.

For each copy sold a £1 will be given to Cancer Research

Table of Plates

Plate 1	The Wood Family 1966	BW-1
Plate 2	Hadyn and Bonny	BW-1
Plate 3	Russell at Pontins 1967	BW-1
Plate 4	River Taff—Pontsticill South Wales 1955	BW-2
Plate 5	Snowden—near Llyn Glaslyn August 1969	BW-2
Plate 6	View from Lee Abbey, N. Devon - Rogers favourite retreat	COL-1
Plate 7	Little Pengelly Cottage The Wood residence 1973 - 1983	COL-1
Plate 8	Rowing Roger - The Gower Peninsula S. Wales 1979	COL-2
Plate 9	Sons Russell and Hadyn 1983	COL-2
Plate 10	Clovelly	COL-3
Plate 11	St. Austell Parish Church ramble Dodman Point.	COL-3
Plate 12	Sarah and Roger	COL-4
Plate 13	Sunset from the Rectory over Braunton Burrows The last photograph Roger ever took.	COL-4
Plate 14	A New Song Coffee Shop - St Austell	BW-3
Plate 15	Roger with Donley Bait	BW-3
Plate 16	Holy Trinity Church - St. Austell	BW-3
Plate 17	Sarah's Ordination to the priesthood	BW-4
Cover photo	Roger taken by Sarah in 2000 Sugar Loaf Mt. Washington State USA	

Except where Roger is in them, all photographs were taken by him.

Plates 4 and 5 are included because of his connections with Wales.
Plate 10 a favourite North Devon Harbour

Table of Contents

Preface	3
Dedication	4
Table of Plates	5
Table of Contents	6
Forward	8
FATHER I WANT TO BE….	9
INDEPENDENCE DAY	9
DEATH.	10
FORGIVEN	10
DILUTED.	11
FEAR	12
GROUNDED	13
KNOTWEED	13
"GETTING TO KNOW YOU"	14
RECLINING.	14
MERCIES – NEEDS AND WANTS	15
NEED A RE-FILL?	15
'REPS' FOR CHRIST.	16
VISION.	16
SPEAK UP FOR HIM!	17
HEALING	18
HEARING	18
SHAME	19
WAIT	20
ACCESS TO THE FATHER	20
BOLD	21
MAKE ME A CHANNEL	22
HANDSFULL	22
"CAN I HAVE MY COLLECTION, MUMMY?'	23
A METHOD OF MEDITATION	23
TRUST	24
IN THE NAME OF JESUS	24
WALKING IN "THE WAY"	25
REMINDER	25
THE WORD	26
"PRAY, THAT YOU MIGHT RECEIVE THE HOLY SPIRIT"	26
EYE TO EYE	27

Table of Contents cont…..

GET RIGHT WITH GOD	27
IMITATORS	28
GRAFTING	28
MOTORWAY BUILDING	29
NEED AN OVERHAUL ?	29
GOSSIP	29
MAYDAY! - MAYDAY! - MAYDAY!	30
SOWING FOR FRUITFULNESS	30
NO ROOM AT THE INN	31
DON'T WASTE THE PASTRY!	31
GET PLOUGHING!	32
THE VALLEY OF THE SHADOW	32
GREAT EXPECTATIONS	33
CONSCIENCE	33
BITE YOUR LIP - OR 'BUTTON IT'!	34
PSALM 22	35
THE DARK SIDE	35
"NO FISHING"	36
PREPARE THE WAY	36
NAVIGATION	37
ON THE ROCK	37
EQUIPPED TO PREPARE	37
MEMORIES	38
LORD, TEACH US TO PRAY	38
VIRGIN BIRTH	39
FORGIVE	39
YOKES	39
IN THE PITS	40
THE LAST WILL AND TESTIMONY	40
APPEARANCES AND DISAPPEARANCES	40
I'LL WALK BESIDE YOU	41
A LIFT UP WITH NO LET DOWN	41
PSALM 46	42
EASTER—A LONG WEEKEND	42
STEPPING STONES OR OPPORTUNITY	43
OPERATION SLATE	43

Forward

Roger Wood died three days before Christmas in 2001 after having been diagnosed with leukaemia 17 years previously. During that time he experienced God's healing in many ways and was able to work alongside me, in the parishes of Illogan in Cornwall and Heanton with Marwood in North Devon, where I continue Rector.

Ever since he was a boy Roger had written doggerels and poems about life in school, the RAF and, more latterly, about the ways in which God speaks in the ordinariness of life.

This anthology is variously humorous, thoughtful and challenging and has come out of a desire to honour Roger's long time desire to share with others how God speaks through everyday situations – and helps us to look at life with open eyes and ears.

Sarah

FATHER I WANT TO BE ………..

Walking in Your way,
Listening to Your voice,
Strengthened by Your power,
Surrounded by Your love,
Embedded in Your truth,
Filled with Your Holy Spirit,
Forgiven by Your grace,
Worthy of Your trust,
Healed by Your wounds,
Fed from Your Word,
Clothed with Your righteousness,
Washed with Your Blood,
Protected by Your armour,
Fit for Your Kingdom,
In Jesus' Name, Amen.

INDEPENDENCE DAY

When was the 'Declaration of Independence?' In the year one - the Fall of Man. And where was the first Garden Centre? Eden. It stocked all sorts of good things; but it also stocked forbidden fruit. It was managed by Adam and Eve Limited - until they got the sack - and then it became an unlimited company when people like you and I joined the staff and continued the mal-practice which the previous owners had begun; until Jesus came . . .

DEATH

Enjoy life to the full. "While we have time, let us do good to all men". (Gal.6:10) - for death will come; but we need have no fear of that, for it is but the gateway to a new life. Those of us who know this, even if we know the Lord and can be sure of His promises, have fleeting doubts and fears. What will death itself be like? I shall be leaving behind those I love - for even if I could take them with me, each one has to face their own personal death. One third of my life is spent in sleep, so why should I fear the sleep which will give way to the most glorious day that I could ever imagine? And even as I get older and my body shows signs of losing its strength, and aches and pains begin to become the common, rather than the uncommon occurrence, why should I be loathe to exchange it for a new body which will not age?

"So will it be with the resurrection of the dead. The body that is sown is perishable, it is raised imperishable. It is sown in dishonour, it is raised in glory; it is sown in weakness, it is raised in power; it is sown a natural body, it is raised a spiritual body".

"Praise be to the God and Father of our Lord Jesus Christ! In His great mercy He has given us new birth into a living hope through the resurrection of Jesus Christ from the dead, and into an inheritance that can never spoil or fade - kept in heaven for you, who through faith are shielded by God's power until the coming of the salvation that is ready to be revealed in the last time" (1.Peter.l:3-5; read on to the end of verse 9). What a super passage of scripture to have read at one's funeral! Why not book it for yours now!

This was indeed read and preached at his Funeral and Thanksgiving Service.

FORGIVEN

When I come before God on the day of judgement, I need have no fear, because I will come hand in hand with Christ who has already forgiven me and will be there to intercede for me before the Father.

So we can be assured of His welcome when we come with Christ and trust in Him. (Eph. 3: 12.)

DILUTED

"That all of them may be one, ...so the world may believe that You have sent Me". John 17;20-21.

We cannot expect the world to believe that the Father sent the Son, or that Jesus' claims are true, unless the world sees something of the reality of the oneness of true Christians.

One example of the travesty and the result of these divisions amongst Christians can be seen in the diversity of opinions about how Religious Education should be taught in schools. That it is being watered down and its truths denied to such an extent that its power is lost and its message becomes ineffectual amidst the demands that other religions are not only factually taught so that their teachings can be recognised for what they are, but that children are also taught and encouraged to take part in the practices and festivals of these other faiths - even to the point of writing prayers to 'foreign gods'.

Leaders of our Churches and Cathedrals go so far as to allow their buildings to be used for multi-faith celebrations and festivals in which the Christian gospel is swept under the carpet and even the Muslim call to prayer is heard coming from the tops of our Cathedral towers and spires.

How Jesus must weep and cry out when His people behave in this way and when those who call themselves Christians allow these things to happen. We not only give the world a false impression of what Christianity is all about, but we hinder people from believing that Jesus Christ is the Son of God and that this gospel is the only true gospel. "That the world may believe that You have sent Me" can hardly be our true prayer if this is the way the Christian Church behaves. It is rather a denial of the truth. No other religion would allow us to present the claims of Jesus Christ to their people in their buildings. Is this the basis of our love for God and our concern for the unity of His Church; the unity of world religions and faiths at the expense of the Christian gospel? The Bible commands us to love our brothers; but the first commandment is to love God and Jesus Christ who He has sent.

FEAR

I have known fear in my life; much of it over-rated and unfounded but, nevertheless, very real to me. On looking back, much of it stemmed from my earliest childhood, through schooling and the second World War into my teens and beyond. There seems to have been an insecurity and a loneliness; my mother's long illness and her own attitude to life may well have been a contributing factor and boarding school did not help. Others could see my fearfulness and played on it, and by my mid-twenties I was ill and feeling unable to cope with my fears any longer. An hour with a psychiatrist was enough for him to detect the problem, if not the root cause. "Why", he asked, "do you keep on saying that you're 'scared stiff'?" Then began the long road back to a position of self-acceptance and of learning to cope and come to terms with my fears and, as my own personal faith increased, so my fears started to recede.

God has spoken to me many times over the years. In one of my most difficult and darkest hours He led me to this verse in Isaiah (41:10) - "So do not fear, for I am with you; do not be dismayed, for I am your God. I will strengthen you and help you; I will uphold you with my righteous (victorious) right hand". And verse 13 - "For I am the Lord your God, who takes hold of your right hand and says to you, 'Do not fear; I will help you'." And those are the verses which have helped me most. They would certainly be in my 'Desert Island' choice.

I have come a long way since those days. In my mid-fifties, when I was diagnosed as having chronic leukaemia, it was the prayers of others, anointing with oil and with the laying on of hands which gave me a peace of heart and mind such that I had never experienced before. About that time God used a Christian writer to give me just the words I needed to support me in my weakness: "All the strength you'll ever need to handle anything is within you now. It was put there by your Creator, who knew very well what you would be up against in this life and has made you equal to it". (Martin Israel).

So I have come to know that "God is able" and that "He is able to keep all that I have committed to Him" until that day when I see Him face to face.

"...but Jesus came and touched them. 'Get up', He said. 'Don't be afraid'. When they looked up, they saw no-one except Jesus". (Matt.17:6-8)

Family Wood - 1966

Hadyn & Bonny

Russell - Pontins 1967

River Taff - Pontsticill. South Wales   1955

Snowdon - near Llyn Glaslyn   August 1969

GROUNDED

I am reminded of the wealth of illustrations that can be used by likening the piloting and flight of an aircraft to the Christian life.

i.e. Am I 'climbing on course', or has somebody pulled my 'undercarriage' switch, preventing me from moving forward without first needing some radical repairs to my framework ?

KNOTWEED

Christ not only died for our sins, but by our sins. Big sins, little sins, unrecognised sins, acknowledged and unacknowledged.

On the wasteland adjoining our garden grows a plant called "Giant Japanese Knotweed". It grows afresh each year and slowly spreads and extends its area. Slowly it has inched its way through the hedge and its shoots are starting to appear in our lawn. "Why don't you get rid of it?", you say. But this is easier said than done. Its roots are shallow and tuberous, but its stems, although thick and apparently strong, are easily broken and break off if an attempt is made to pull them up. Even if they are dug up, the smallest root particle left in the soil will sprout and grow again: so you can see that its removal from the site is very difficult and its total eradication almost impossible. We have been told that it is considered to be such a threat to the land that the law insists that it should be dug up and burnt on site and that removal from the site is prohibited.

Isn't this so like the sins that grow within us and around us to pull us down and trip us up? Man is sinful by nature, and just when we think we have overcome it, it will spring up again or another one will raise its ugly head elsewhere. We can never be truly free from sin. If that were possible, Jesus would have had no need to die for us. But He did! And we read in 1 John 1:8 that "if we say that we have no sin, the truth is not in us: but if we confess our sins, He is faithful and just and will forgive us our sins and cleanse us from every kind of wrong".

"And none, O Lord, have perfect rest, for none are wholly free from sin; and they who fain would serve you best, are conscience most of wrong within".

"GETTING TO KNOW YOU"

If we want to get to know someone, we will make every effort to please them and to spend much time in their company. Many Christians are still only 'engaged' to God - they have gone no further, but sit on the 'observation platform'. This is not knowing God; it is just knowing about God. We get to know God through His grace; and the greatest demonstration to us of His grace is the gift to us of His Son. For it is through the Son that we really see and get to know the Father. Jesus says, "He who has seen Me has seen the Father". Philip said to Him, "Lord, show us the Father". And Jesus replied, "Have you been so long with Me and yet you ask, Show us the Father?"

Father, I want always to be seeking to know more of You. I need a personal introduction; Jesus has already given me the invitation - and at the bottom are the letters R.S.V.P. He is saying - 'Come to Me and meet My Father.

"There is no-one like You, O Lord; and there is no God but You, as we have heard with our own ears".

"O Lord God Almighty, who is like You? You are mighty, O Lord, and Your faithfulness surrounds You". (Ps.89:8)

"Home-build in the Spirit now, and the waiting-time will be well spent". (God Calling)

RECLINING

Father, I want to love You so much that I may have the privilege of reclining next to You. Being so close to You that I may hear Your every word. Leaning on You, that I may become a part of You. For when I lean against something or someone, it means that I trust them to support me and hold me up. A trust that knows that You will not let me down. That You don't play tricks and move out of the way so that I end up on the floor.

Lord, I trust You; I do trust You. To be sure that I walk along Your path, lead me as the shepherd leads his sheep. To hear You and to be obedient when You say "Follow Me".

MERCIES – NEEDS AND WANTS

I am reminded of how much and how many things we take for granted. We accept them without so much as 'batting an eyelid' until something goes wrong or just doesn't happen in the way we expect it to. Life itself, sight, hearing, touch, taste, smell (our senses) and our general health, friendships, marriage, our waking and the faithful arrival of each day, the joy of birthdays, Christmas and what it truly means and commemorates; even the weather - especially if its wet and we would like it to be fine because it spoils our pleasure. And that leads on to selfishness. What we want as opposed to what we need. We would like endless days of glorious summer weather, while the farmer is crying out for rain. We grumble at a hosepipe ban or when the flow from our taps becomes a trickle. We cannot but admit that we take too much for granted and that our thankfulness when things are running smoothly, in no way matches our grumbles and complaints when things go wrong.

"All things come from You, O Lord...". "Your mercies are new every morning; great is Your faithfulness".

O Give thanks to the Lord all you His people;

O Give thanks to the Lord for He is good.

'Let us praise, let us shout; Let us celebrate and dance. O Give thanks to the Lord for He is good.'

NEED A RE-FILL?

A jug that has been filled with water does not stay full to the brim - some evaporates. A kettle that is 'on the boil' does not remain full. Some of the contents evaporate. To be full again, more water must be added.

So it is with the Holy Spirit; we need re-filling - topping up from time to time.

Make me open to this Lord, ready to receive a rich infilling of Your Holy Spirit and open to whatever gifts You wish to give me. In Jesus' Name. Amen.

'REPS' FOR CHRIST

"All men will know that you are my disciples if you have love one for another". John 13:35.

Jesus turns to the world and says: "On the basis of my authority, I give you the right to judge whether this person is a Christian or not, on the evidence of the love they show to other Christians".

What non-Christians say about us behind our backs is often a truer reflection of what they really think of us, than what they are prepared to say to our faces. So, if someone says to you, "You are not a true Christian because you talk and gossip about other Christians"; and if it's true, you have no right to be angry; but rather you should come before God and ask Him to forgive you for failing to represent Him faithfully and in the way He has commanded you.

This does not mean, however, that we are not Christians, but that we are failing in that part of our responsibility as Christians and have mis-represented Him in front of non-Christians. For this, we can always make amends and try to do better.

O Lord, kindle and fan all my weak loves into flame and make me afire with Your love. Amen.

VISION

Our 'field of vision' is limited, but God's vision is all enveloping, He can see the whole. So it's important that what we can see is only of Him, and that anything within our vision that is not of Him be removed. Then He can replace it with the part of His vision that at this time we cannot see, because it is clouded and pushed out by our own thoughts and ideas about what His vision for us should be. No pre-conceived ideas on our part, but only ideas conceived in Him. Vision, therefore, is imagination + purpose, inspired by the Holy Spirit.

SPEAK UP FOR HIM!

"As I have loved you, so you must love one another".

What a challenge! And how far short of it I fall. How often I fail to display that love by not speaking up for Him. By denying Him - not in the word, but in the silence. How many opportunities have I missed by not speaking for Him or about Him; not acknowledging Him. There is a verse in scripture in which Jesus says - "He who acknowledges me before men, I will acknowledge before my Father in heaven". Matt. 10:32.

If Jesus had to write a reference for me - and one day I shall be expecting Him to do so - what will He write? 'This man is found wanting in that he does not speak up for me'? If this is so, why, I ask myself? Am I ashamed of my Lord? Am I more frightened of men than I am of Him? What place does He have in my life"?

A shy person misses out on so much in life. One does not have to be brazen to be bold. "In quietness and in confidence shall be your strength" (Is.30:15.). I need to be confident and to step out in His strength. Provided I am walking in the will of God, I need not, I should not, be afraid of what people may say about me. So, 'Be bold, be strong, for the Lord your God is with you'. Ask the Holy Spirit to strengthen your resolve to speak out for Him.

'Jesus, confirm my heart's desire to work and think and speak for Thee; So may I grasp the holy fire, And still stir up the gift in me'. He said;

> "Freely, freely, you have received; Freely, freely give
> Go in My Name and because you believe,
> Others will know that I live".

If we go in His Name, and speak in His Name, we have His backing and need not fear what mere man can do to us. For "in the Name of Jesus every knee shall bow and every tongue confess that Jesus Christ is Lord, to the glory of God the Father."

"May the Lord make your love increase and overflow for each other and for everyone else, just as ours does for you".1 Thess. 3:12.

"Now that you have purified yourselves by obeying the truth so that you have sincere love for your brothers, love one another deeply, from the heart". 1.Pet.1:22.

HEALING

It would seem that there are three ways in which Jesus healed.

1. Through the forgiveness of sin - the physical symptoms were not indicative of the primary cause. The root problem was sin and what was required was that the person had faith to receive what JESUS had to offer - the forgiveness of their sins, and then the physical symptoms went and they were healed.

2. Through the faith and prayers of those who brought the sick to Jesus.

3. Through a miraculous intervention by Jesus - sometimes irrespective of the person's faith - but with the command "Go, and sin no more".

Sometimes the person was told to do something which would demonstrate their faith in Jesus' power to heal - "Get up", "Go", etc. Sometimes Jesus asked why they'd come or what they wanted. At other times the person was so ill or demon-possessed that Jesus just looked, saw, had compassion on them and healed them or cast the demon out.

HEARING

Job said, "My ears had heard of You; but now my eyes have seen You". Job. 42: 5. Many people - even some of those in our churches - have heard of God, but they do not hear Him. They need a revelation - a revealing, so that they hear God speaking to them personally; not just hear of Him. I have heard of lots of people that I do not know personally because I have never met them. And because I have never met them, there is no relationship; no personal contact; no love, no commitment; just a vague recollection of having heard something about them.

Father, help me to know You more clearly; to love You more dearly and to follow You more nearly (closely), day by day. Amen.

SHAME

It is to my shame, yet I know it to be true of many - even in Biblical times and in the days of the young Churches, that the times when I feel closest to the Lord, most attentive to Him and, yes, even hearing Him most clearly, are those when I am sick or at my lowest ebb. And when all seems right with the world and I am on top and should be full of praise and thanksgiving, I often spend less time with Him. There have been times when I have almost forgotten or ignored Him and my Quiet Time has been rushed and almost a formality. What must He think of me then? It must make Him sad. Yet, when next I cry out to Him, He is always there to comfort, help encourage - even heal, or gives me strength to bear my passing difficult circumstances or situation. He bears no grudges and ignores my unworthiness.

I am reminded of Paul when he says, "The good that I would, I do not; but the evil that I would not, that I do".

So forgive me, Lord. My nature is such that I admit that You will have to do so again and again. Help me to make that daily commitment to walk with You, listen for Your voice and be obedient to Your Word; for when I do so, I feel that I have achieved something; not only for myself, but because I know that I have pleased You.   Amen.

> Not for the hope of gaining aught,
> Not seeking a reward;
> But as Thyself hast loved me,
> O Ever Loving Lord.
>
> So I would love Thee, dearest Lord,
> And in Thy praise will sing,
> Only because Thou art my God
> And my most loving King.

WAIT

"Wait" is the word I believe God has shown me in my reading this morning. I had a picture of someone waiting for a bus. When it is due, we begin to look for it with anticipation, but as the time of its arrival passes and it does not come into view, we start looking at our watches. Then, as the minutes tick by, we begin to become impatient. Perhaps we pace up and down or stamp our feet. Then we begin to get annoyed - even angry - and eventually lose faith that it is going to arrive at all and turn away from the bus stop in despair. As we do this the bus comes round the corner and all our stress and disappointment melt away as we settle down in our seat and the warmth and comfort replace the cold and draughtiness of that inhospitable bus shelter.

Waiting isn't easy. It tests our patience and sometimes the Lord may make us wait to do just that. Whether it's the bus or the friend who is late; the traffic lights at the roadworks which turn red as we approach just when we are in a hurry; the letter in the post or the phone call from a friend.

God makes us wait too; for there are three answers to prayer that He can give us. Yes - that is within My will - go ahead. No - that plan of action is not in your best interests. Wait - it is not time yet, I want to show you something - to teach you something; I have another plan which is better; that course of action would be dangerous, there are other factors which you need to consider before making a decision; what you are considering might be harmful to others and I need time to show you that in a way that you will be able to understand and accept.

Wait can be the caution of God's traffic lights. Wait for the caution to change to Go before you move in the way He directs.

ACCESS TO THE FATHER

"Through Jesus Christ" - what does this mean; relief at the end of someone's long prayer? Or much more. The only way to the Father - The Gate to the Sheepfold - The Cross - The veil of the Temple - The blood of Jesus - all that Jesus Christ has done for us to gain access to the Father - to Eternal Life!

BOLD

BOLD - the opposite of timid.

Press the bold button on my word processor and the words stand out - are easily read. Press the shift-lock on the typewriter and it produces capital letters which make the message plain for all to see. Both actions demand more than "wishful thinking". They need a positive act of will on our part - to press the button and to want to see the result.

"Fan into flame the gift God has given you". (2,Tim.1:6)

Don't be timid about it. (2.Tim.1:7) or ashamed to testify (2.Tim.1:8) Is my face radiant because I have spoken with the Lord? (Exod.34:29)

Do I cover my face with a veil so that others cannot see what I have experienced? Moses didn't put the veil over his face until after he had finished speaking to the people, so that they could see the radiance on his face and realise where he had been and what he had seen was 'for real' - like the Sanhedrin who 'took notice of them that they had been with Jesus'. (Acts 4:13) Note Peter and John's courage - boldness. The glory which was on Moses' face faded, but the glory of the new covenant - our righteousness and our hope in Christ - remains. For when anyone turns to Christ, the veil is taken away to reveal His Glory. And since we have such a hope, we are very bold (2.Cor.3:12) and the result of this boldness is seen in verse 18 which speaks of reflection, transformation, likeness.

Lord, transform us into your likeness, so that we may reflect Your Glory,

Amen.

BOLD or bowled? Face up, Eye on the ball, a straight bat.

Compare the Batsman's equipment with the Christian's Armour:-

1. Box/Guard – Belt
2. Body Shield – Breastplate
3. Boots (well studded) – Sandals
4. Pads - Shield
5. Bat - Sword.
6. Helmet - Helmet

MAKE ME A CHANNEL

"Not everything I say to you is for others. Yes, you are a channel through which My love can flow; but I want to remove, to burn away the dross, the sediment which lines the walls of that channel, so that which passes through it on its way to others does not become tainted in the passing, but arrives with them as pure as it was when it left me".

This is what the Lord said to me when I prayed that I could be 'a channel through which His love could flow'.

So what sediment lines the walls of my channel? Self-seeking, pride, often unspoken annoyance at other people's attitudes, yet not prepared to accept criticism myself, lack of self-control, laziness . . .

Enough to make a start on. Lord, help me to do something about it- NOW!

HANDSFULL

"Nothing in my hands I bring . . ." "What can I give Him, poor as I am?" . . "Give my heart".

So often when we approach God our hands are full of burdens, cares, requests, "shopping lists" and the prayer begins 'please I want'. What we don't hold out to Him is ourselves. There is no room for this in our hands or even tucked under our arms. It is only when we come to Him with open empty hands, offering ourselves and nothing more - for we have nothing acceptable to give Him - that He can fill our hands - open, empty, ready to receive - with the power and resources which He longs to give us. Some of these things may not be the things we think we need, but that He, in His infinite wisdom and discernment, knows we have need of.

Father, You long to give me so much, but my hands are always full. Help me to empty them so that I can receive the gifts which You long to give me. In Jesus' Name. Amen.

View from Lee Abbey, N Devon - Rogers favourite retreat

Little Pengelly Cottage - the Wood residence 1973 -1983

Rowing Roger - the Gower Peninsula S. Wales					1979

Rogers sons Russell and Hadyn					1983

Clovelly

St. Austell Parish Church Ramble - Dodman Point 1990

Sarah and Roger

Roger's last photograph - Sunset from Rectory over Braunton Burrows

"CAN I HAVE MY COLLECTION, MUMMY?'

"David said to him, 'Let me have the site of your threshing floor so that I can build an altar to the Lord, that the plague on the people may be stopped. Sell it to me at the full price'.

"Araunah said to David, 'Take it! Let my Lord the King do whatever pleases him. Look I will give the oxen for the burnt offerings, the threshing sledges for the wood, and the wheat for the grain offering. I will give all this'.

"But King David replied to Araunah, 'No, I insist on paying the full price'. I will not take for the Lord what is yours, or sacrifice a burnt offering which costs me nothing".

Perhaps this is where we go wrong in bringing up our children. We give them pocket money and then when Sunday comes and they ask us for 'money for the collection', we give it to them without batting an eyelid. So they don't learn at this early stage the meaning of sacrificial giving, because they never have to give sacrificially of what is their own.

A METHOD OF MEDITATION

Take a verse from the Bible or a hymn and divide it into words or phrases. Allow time and thought to dwell on each and for the Holy Spirit to reveal its meaning by showing you other words or verses which relate to it. Example - "JESUS IS LORD".

Jesus - my Saviour - the Perfect Man - the Perfect Lover - My Example - He died for me - that I might live - Name above all names - The very thought of Thee etc.

Is - is the same yesterday, today and for ever - Here now - Present - Emmanuel etc.

Lord - My God - Rabboni - Master - Of all - My All etc.

Is He My Lord, My God, My All? - Spend some time meditating on this.

TRUST

There is nothing more humbling; nothing that more brings to light our degree of trust in God, in Jesus or in the power of the Holy Spirit - or our lack of it - than when we are faced with a situation over which we have no control; something over which we have no choice and from which we have no escape.

This is why I am sure I would be a very poor subject for hypnotism; why the thought of an anaesthetic or an operation - even death, instils fear and apprehension into the hearts and minds of so many of us. Somehow it is easier to cope with death because it's inevitable for us all, and I know that Jesus is going to be there with me and I shall meet Him at last. But with the other instances, I suppose it's fear of something going wrong and of one not being in control of oneself. Self, yes, that word rears its ugly head again - not totally dead and handed over to God. It's like the fear which one experiences at the onset of an epileptic fit - knowing its happening and not being able to do anything about it.

So we are back to "trust". And its not until I am able to humble myself and put myself and my life totally and unreservedly into the hands of God, that these fears will melt away. Meanwhile they mar and spoil my Christian life and witness. But when I allow Jesus to set me free, I shall be free indeed.

Hallelujah!

IN THE NAME OF JESUS

The power of His Name. Able to break down strongholds - to protect us from the evil one. To keep us safe. The Name is JESUS. JESUS. Pray in His Name, Work in His Name, Live in His Name, Go forth in His Name, seek protection in His Name. Worship His Name.

JESUS - At the Name of Jesus every knee shall bow. Love His Name. Love Jesus. Repeat His Name. Become familiar with the Person of His Name. JESUS - Saviour - Redeemer - Lord - Master - Rabboni. Praise His Name. Praise the Lord Jesus. Glorify His Name.

John 17;11,12,15.

WALKING IN "THE WAY"

Walking
  along the way
    on the mountain top
      through the valley
        alone
          with a companion
            beside someone
              ahead
                behind - dragging or following
                  tall
                    with measured pace
                      in silence
                        and talking
                          uphill
                            and downhill
                              slowly
                                and fast
                                  with a wonder
                                    on air
                                      in His Master's steps
                                      back to happiness.
                                      Home at last!

R.L.W.

REMINDER

If you are one of those people who like to sign their letters - 'in the Lord' or 'in Christ Jesus'; remember the implied prefix - 'I AM A BELIEVER'.

THE WORD

Father, thank you for Your Word. Thank you that each time we read it, we can glean new insight, new knowledge, new awareness and new truths about You. Thank you that it teaches us so much about You, Father; so much about Jesus and so much about the power of Your Holy Spirit which is available to us.

Father, protect Your Word for it is so precious to us. May we always be free to open its pages and to learn more of You and of Your love for us; to learn more of Jesus so that our lives may reflect His Glory and to learn more of Your Holy Spirit's power so that in Your strength we may live lives more worthy of You and all that You want us to be. We ask in Jesus' precious Name. Amen.

"PRAY, THAT YOU MIGHT RECEIVE THE HOLY SPIRIT"

Spirit of the living God -

BREAK ME -	as one would break up a jelly into pieces.
MELT ME -	as the boiling water melts the jelly, breaking down all the pieces that have been torn apart, so that my whole being is subjected to Your Will.
MOULD ME -	as the jelly is poured into a mould; so may my life be poured into Your mould and become all that You want it to be.
FILL ME -	with the presence and power of Your Holy Spirit. Fill me, Lord, right up to the top, so that as I 'gel', I may become - not the hard, square, lump of a thing that I used to be; wrapped up in an airtight skin and sitting on the shelf, a lifeless, artificially coloured object - but living and vibrant and free. Ready for use. Someone You can take and use at any time to promote Your Kingdom and bring You Glory.

Spirit of the living God, fall afresh on me.

Amen.

EYE TO EYE

2 Chronicles 7:14 talks about seeking God's face. Eye to eye contact. If I find that I am unable to do this, there is something wrong. Am I ashamed or trying to hide something? What have I done wrong? If I humble myself, confess any wrong and pray for forgiveness, He will gently lift up my head until my eyes meet His. Then I will meet Him face to face, see the love in His eyes and know that I am forgiven.

GET RIGHT WITH GOD

If God were to show me "the number of my days" (Psalm 39:4) - to tell me that I only had a month to live, what would be my reaction? Would I crawl into a corner and mope and cry the time away, or would each day, each hour, each minute take on a new value and a greater importance? Would there be places I would want to visit, things I would want to do, people I would want to see - possibly get right with, attitudes in my life that I would wish to change, things that I had done in the past for which I would want to seek forgiveness and others that I would wish to set in order, so that those left behind to settle my affairs would not suffer on my account?

Way back, I can remember attending a series of meetings at the Royal Albert Hall in London entitled "Get Right with God". Perhaps I would want to use the time to establish a closer walk with Him before I met Him face to face.

As individuals we would all have different values and priorities if we knew that our time was limited. Limited either because He sends for us to go and stay in one of those mansions that He talks of preparing for us, or because the time has arrived for Him to come again to receive to Himself. "For we do not know the day or the hour when the Son of man will come" or when our life will be required of us. We are just told to be ready. Am I ? Are you?

IMITATORS

Living the Christian life does not have to be complicated. The rules are straight forward, clear and simple. What God requires is our obedience (Micah 6:8). Ephesians 5 gives some guidelines. Following them is far easier than trying to find loop-holes and skate around them. We are told to be "imitators" - that means following closely the example of the Master. To live a life as He did. To have no truck with anything which has a hint of immorality. To live as children of the light in goodness, righteousness and truth. Watch your tongue "for it is shameful even to mention what the disobedient do in secret" (v.12). Be wise, not foolish. Give thanks to God; submit to one another in reverence to Christ. Live by the Spirit, worthy of your calling in Christ. Purified from sin by the Blood of Jesus.

GRAFTING

". . . if the root is holy, so are the branches" (Romans 11:16)

If you have been grafted in among the others and now share in the nourishing sap from the olive root, do not boast over those branches. If you do, consider this - you do not support the root, but the root supports you. Branches were broken off (because of unbelief) so that you could be grafted in (vs 17-19). You stand by faith. Don't be arrogant, but afraid. If God didn't spare the natural branches, He will not spare you either. Because if God, through His kindness, was able to graft you in, He is equally able to cut you out and to graft in the original branches if they no longer persist in unbelief (vs 22-23 paraphrased). "Let him that standeth take heed lest he fall".

I believe these verses could be applied to those involved in second marriages and the children of each party who have been 'grafted in' from the first marriage; and their relationships with one another. A situation that can be either painful or joyful.

MOTORWAY BUILDING

How did John the Baptist prepare the way for Jesus? What word did he get from the prophet Isaiah?

Prepare the way! Fill in the valleys! Flatten the hills and mountains! Straighten the crooked roads And smooth the rough ones!

Then - when all is ready

"All men will see the salvation of our God".

Let's join the gang and help prepare a Highway for Our God!

NEED AN OVERHAUL?

1. Service the system
2. Sweep the chimney
3. Rake out the ashes
4. Get out the poker
5. Stoke the boiler
6. Put on more fuel
7. Open up the damper
8. Fan the flame

a) Fill the oil reservoir
b) Trim the wick

GOSSIP

Cut out gossiping about people's faults and failings; or even mentioning them. You find this difficult? God sees them all - yours and mine too - and He is quite capable of sorting them out. He uses conscience and a willing obedient heart.

"What do you want?" he asks. "Lord, make me clean."

"Be thou clean", He replies.

"For it is shameful even to mention what the disobedient do in secret". Eph.5:12.

MAYDAY! - MAYDAY! - MAYDAY!

When you are flying a Jet aircraft and running out of fuel, you have got to do three things -

(1) Act fast.

(2) Keep your head.

(3) Seek assistance in finding somewhere to land.

The amount of fuel left in your tanks is referred to in terms of time - in minutes - and called 'endurance'.

Endurance 4 - 30 minutes Endurance 3 - 20 minutes Endurance 2 - 10 minutes Endurance 1 - you are literally 'flying on air' with empty tanks!

I don't believe we should reach that stage. We should have asked for help long before then. God gives us help and patience to endure, but He expects us to ask for it, to listen to His directions and to follow them.

SOWING FOR FRUITFULNESS

Some thoughts on the meaning of the 'Parable of the Sower'. Which category do I fall into - or onto what sort of ground does my seed fall?

In just the same way as the farmer experiences good and bad crops from one year to another, so our yield and our fruitfulness will vary from year to year as we grow or cease to grow in our Christian life. We can't blame the sower for the ground on which the seed falls. If we haven't tilled, ploughed, harrowed, removed the rocks etc. then the resulting crop will vary in its yield and quality. And even if we believe that our soil is good and that we have good and noble hearts that hear the word and retain it, we are warned that only by perseverance (tribulation) will we produce a good crop - "... because we know that suffering produces perseverance; perseverance, character, and character, hope". The biblical word 'tribulation' has its root meaning in the word 'thresh' - a process that applies to Christians as well as to wheat. Threshing separates the wheat from the chaff, and the end product is what Jesus uses to enrich our lives.

NO ROOM AT THE INN

No room at the inn; No Room, No Room!
My unborn Saviour rejected so soon.
Despised and rejected from manger to tree,
Where He died and He suffered for you and for me.
Is it nothing to you, as you pass him by?
Was it worth being born in that manger to lie?
Do I care that He lived in this world of contempt,
Not wanted by people to whom He was sent?
People no different to you, or from me;
Each born with a choice, freewill and a key
To the door that He asks us to open to Him.
Will you say, "Lord, of course there's room. Come in!'

DON'T WASTE THE PASTRY !

If you are making pastry for Jam tarts, you roll it out on the board and then press out the circles of pastry with a cutter. When you have removed these and put them into a baking tin, you are left with a lot of irregular scrappy pieces of pastry which, to some, might appear to be useless. But if you gather them up in your hands and kneed them into a ball, you can then roll it out again and press out enough circles to make several more tarts - even repeating the process until nothing is wasted.

So when I feel 'all cut up' and of no use to anyone, am I saying that I am not prepared to allow God to remould 'my remainders' and to prepare me for the next act? He can use remainders and turn 'weaknesses into opportunities'!

Lord, make me willing to be 'remoulded' - like a tyre, and given extra life. Amen.

GET PLOUGHING!

Both Jeremiah 4:3 and Hosea 10:12 invoke us to sow righteousness for our-selves and to break up our unploughed ground. For it is time to seek the Lord until He comes and showers righteousness on us. Then we will reap the fruit of unfailing love.

If our spiritual harvest wasn't particularly good this year, we have got to work harder for the Lord our Righteousness so that we reap a more fruitful harvest for next year. Holiness becomes His house for ever. When the farmer ploughs, he sets his eye on a point in the hedge on the far side of the field and 'goes for it'. Prepare the ground, plough straight and deep, and you will reap the increase in God's time. His harvest season starts with the plough!

THE VALLEY OF THE SHADOW

"The valley of the shadow" might be a good description of bereavement. The deeper the valley, the longer the shadow. But no valley, however long and deep, is endless. There is a way in and a way out. Allow God to guide you through it, then you won't be pacing up and down in it, because the Lord who is your Shepherd will lead you through it and comfort you along the way, protecting you from all evil.

There is nearly always a stream in the valley. If it is not of water, it will be of your tears. Let them flow. They will be for your healing - the waters of comfort.

With the Shepherd in front, you following, and His goodness and mercy with you each and every day, you will come out of the shadow into the light again, letting go of your loved one so that they may 'dwell in the house of the Lord for ever'. (Psalm 23)

"I know the one in whom I trust and I am sure that He is able to guard safely all that I have given to Him until the day of His return".

(2. Tim. 1-12)

"May our Lord Jesus Christ Himself and God Our Father, who has loved us and given us everlasting comfort and hope which we don't deserve, comfort your hearts with all comfort, and help you in every good thing you say and do". (2.Thes.2:16-1?.)

A New Song Coffee Shop—St Austell   1981

Roger with Donkey bait    Holy Trinity Church - St Austell

Sarah's Ordination as priest

GREAT EXPECTATIONS

"Great Expectations" produce not repeat performances of the past, but new experiences of Him. If we go into a situation that we have been in before without expecting to get something new out of it, we won't be disappointed! But we may well miss the thing that God wants to show us, to enrich our lives with, and we shall return that much poorer and God will be disappointed. Look alive! Be alert! God does not 'pull His cabbages twice'! As Joni puts it in her book "SECRET STRENGTH" -

"If nature waits on tiptoe for the coming of Jesus (Romans 8:19), you and I shouldn't be caught flat-footed".

CONSCIENCE

Recently I saw again in our High Street the small hunched figure of the little man who appears from time to time throughout the year to solicit a meagre supplement to his all too slender means by selling, or trying to sell, whatever he has grown in his small garden or collected from the hedgerows - a few small straggly lettuces in summer, small plastic bags of blackberries in the Autumn, but at Christmas he has only himself to give, and in a weak and broken voice he sings carols from a well-worn carol sheet as he extends his greasy cloth cap to those who pass him by. I saw him and passed him by too. Then my conscience struck me and I returned to search for him, but he had gone.

Two days later I was given a second chance and put something in his cap. I mumbled "Happy Christmas" and moved on.

Perhaps you are like me sometimes. You'll give but not want to be involved and, conscience appeased, we go upon our way. We do not want to run the risk of being involved; commitment frightens us.

Yet Lord, I often spurn lack of commitment in others whilst, as you have revealed, I have not completely conquered lack of commitment in myself. Thank you, Lord, for revealing it to me. Help me to overcome this in Your strength and with Your love. Amen.

BITE YOUR LIP - OR 'BUTTON IT'!

"Be slow to anger", the Bible tells us. 'Count to ten', some advise - or beyond if necessary! Bite your lip or 'button it'! Acknowledging our anger helps us to control it. Then assume responsibility for the anger. It is not what has been said or done which has made us angry, but our reaction to it. We make a conscious choice to be angry and the choice hinges on the way we react to what has caused the situation. We may feel that anger is justified - a justifiable reaction - righteous anger. We should not lose control but rather explain what has made us feel the way we do and then admit to the person concerned our feelings of bitterness. Even if these are expressed with strong feeling (controlled expression), they will not hurt the other party; providing that we make it clear that we have accepted responsibility for the way we feel. When our motive for our actions is expressed in concern that the other person should understand how we feel, rather than in anger over what has occurred, we stand a better chance of speedy reconciliation, instead of letting the wound fester and "allowing the sun to go down upon our wrath". In all events, make amends before you leave that person - or by bedtime. Then our relationship stands a better chance of working in the way that God designed.

Have a look at Luke 24:13-35 - the walk to Emmaus. Jesus, who had just been through so much, could easily have 'lost His cool' with these two men - and with doubting Thomas too. But instead He was gentle with them; reminding them of the prophecies and what had been foretold in the scriptures. He did not 'blow His stack' or 'lose His cool'. He continued to walk with them, explaining what had happened and then cemented the relationship by accepting their offer of hospitality - instead of going off in a huff. And when they recognised Him, He forestalled their embarrassment and left. He didn't have to say - "Now go and tell the others what you have seen. He could trust them to do that for Him - before they even went to bed!

Are you harbouring a grudge? Is there anyone you need to get right with; someone you are angry with and need to apologise to? "Get rid of all bitterness, rage and anger, brawling and slander, along with every form of malice" (Eph.4:31). "Forgive one another; even as Christ forgave you" (Col.4:13).

PSALM 22

Psalm 22 gives us a 'true to life' illustration of what it must have felt like to die on a cross. It is almost prophetic and includes some of our Lord's words from the cross. Verses 1-21 paint a picture in the mind of the cruelty, pain and loneliness of a lingering death and provide us with a thought provoking meditation of what Jesus endured for each one of us.

But it does not end at verse 21; anymore than Jesus' life ended at the words "Into Your hands I commit My Spirit". Verses 22 onwards remind us of the victory of the cross and of the life beyond the grave. The last few words are those of accomplishment and hope for all - "for He has done it!" Hallelujah!

THE DARK SIDE

Do stressful situations bring out in you a side of your nature that you would prefer other people should not know about?

This morning, while I was still in bed, the phone rang. It was a neighbour asking me to move my car so that the coal lorry could get past along the narrow lane outside our house. Reminiscent of war-time air raid warnings, I slipped trousers and an anorak on over my pyjamas and shoes onto bare feet, grabbed the car keys and went to move it. The car would not start! After enlisting the help of a neighbour to push it and eventually "bump starting" it down a slope, I returned home to reflect on the sort of thoughts that had been going through my mind during the past half-hour. They were not very Christian!

Cars are fine when they go, but when they don't, I know of few other situations in our modem day living - blocked drains is another! - which send Christian thoughts - and sometimes behaviour and language - to the wind and this reveals something of what is under the thin veneer of our Christian standards.

On turning to my Bible reading for the day I found these words - "Give your burdens to the Lord. He will carry them He will not permit the godly to slip or fall. Don't worry about things - food, drink, money, clothes" - and cars? "Your Heavenly Father already knows perfectly well that you need them". (Psalm 55:22; Matthew 26: 25 and 32).

"NO FISHING"

What did Jesus do for us on the Cross? When we were dead in our sins God made us alive with Christ. How? He forgave us our sins, took them away and nailed them to the Crass. We sing "Lift High The Cross" so that others can see what God has done for us in Jesus. But sometimes, instead of doing that, we busy ourselves with a large pair of pliers trying to pull out the nails so that we can wallow in our sins again - like trying to take down that sign that reads "No Fishing" so that we can poach and weigh ourselves down again with all the sins which He died to remove

And I am no saint! I write to convince myself as much as to help others. Sometimes believing is a jolly sight easier than practising what you believe!

Isn't this where God's grace comes in? Jesus swept the room and then He cleared up the mess. The carpenter's shop was left tidy when He had finished His job. When He had shaped the pieces of wood, He gathered up the shavings. What does our floor look like when we've finished a job?

PREPARE THE WAY

We have to prepare ourselves, not sit back and expect God to do it for us. It's called love, caring, pleasing, obedience. Being wise and not foolish virgins; trimming our lamps and having oil in reserve. Trimmed lamps burn brighter; pruned trees produce more fruit.

We sing "O Come, O Come, Immanuel", but have we prepared the way for the Lord? What allegiance do we have for a King? What respect, when we expect Him to approach us with bare feet along a dusty road? Is He not worthy of our consideration, preparation, exaltation - the red carpet, royal welcome? It's not only what He is prepared to do for us, but what we are prepared to do for Him!

NAVIGATION

Navigation consists, in a large part, of travelling from one known point to another; whether it be a landmark or a seamark. Sometimes these points are too far apart to be seen visually the one from the other and we have to concentrate on a navigational aid. This can be the stars, a sextant, a compass, or the signal from a light or beacon. We have only to take our eyes off the instrument panel for a brief period or cease to listen to the signal on our radio and we will find ourselves starting to drift off course.

If we want to arrive safely at our destination, we have to watch and to listen continually. What does this tell me about my Christian life?

ON THE ROCK

Are we on the rock or in the water? Are we being thrown and beaten against the rocks by the rough waters of life, or have we discovered the Rock of our salvation which is able to protect us from this?

Many a rock has a fortress on top of it - Gibraltar, Tintagel, Edinburgh Castle, St. Michael's Mount, Lindisfarne. Jesus tells us the story of the man who built his house upon the rock and the man who unwisely built upon the sand. If we are floundering in the water and turn to Him and call Him by name, He is about to save us - to throw us a lifeline, lift us out of the rough waters and set our feet firmly upon the Rock. Then we must hold on to the Rock - or we will "back-slide" into the sea again. By faith we are saved.

EQUIPPED TO PREPARE

We are told that John the Baptist wore a belt. He almost certainly wore sandals. He came proclaiming 'the truth' and with 'his feet shod with the preparation of the Gospel of peace'. God had equipped him with at least two parts of the 'armour of God' which he needed for 'proclaiming the way of the Lord'. And, since Scripture gives no indication to the contrary, he was almost certainly protected with the rest of the armour of God as well - with which he would be able to overcome 'all the fiery darts of the evil one'.

MEMORIES

Father, thank you for all the good and pleasant memories of my childhood. Help me to bring to the surface and to leave at the foot of the cross all that was hurtful in that area of my life. Help me to put away childish things and to replace them with the maturity of adulthood and to trust You, Jesus, with the management of my life. Show me the truth about myself and how to relate to others and show me the things that spoil my relationship with others. I want to have done with them. I was not in control when I acted in that way; the little child within me was pushing me along.

So wash me clean, Lord, and till my life with the maturity of Your Holy Spirit, because I ask this in Jesus' Name. Amen.

"Break up your unploughed ground and do not sow among thorns. Circumcise yourselves to the Lord ... " (Jer.4:3-4).

LORD, TEACH US TO PRAY

Perhaps teaching others to pray can best be done by praying aloud with them. By showing them that although there are times and occasions for formal prayers, that the times when we can build up the closest relationship with God is when we talk to Him as a friend through Jesus. Not with any rehearsal or 'highfaluting' words, but just naturally, as though He was in the room with us - because He is; and I am sure He values our own faltering words far more than something written by somebody else in a book.

So let's have a conversation with Him. That means allowing Him time to speak to us too? Don't be afraid of the silences, the times when you are trying to think of what to say next. He can use those times to speak to you - a still small voice - listen for it! God has given us two ears and one mouth. We need to listen for twice as long as we pray. I'm not good at that, but if He can't get a word in edgeways, how can He speak and how shall we hear Him? Prayer is two-way traffic - up to heaven and 'down to earth'. Relax - Relate - Receive - Respond.

VIRGIN BIRTH

Women in this country who want a child, but have no desire for the love or the cares and responsibilities of marriage, are having a baby by artificial insemination and calling the process 'virgin birth'. Yet there has only been one Virgin Birth since the world began. That of a Saviour, born of God, conceived by the Holy Spirit, born to a virgin, Mary. Born, not by artificial insemination with the sperm of a human donor; but inseminated by the Spirit of God to a woman chosen and set apart for that purpose - God's purpose - to give birth to Jesus. The only truly Virgin Birth that was and ever more will be. Never to be repeated; for God did it all, in Mary and through the Holy Spirit. Only a God-fathered child can be of Virgin Birth.

FORGIVE

Is this you? Have you a Christian friend with whom you need to get right before God? Face the situation, forget your pride, forgive the hurt. As you make your peace with them you will make peace with God.

Keep short accounts with one another. Submit to one another in love and "let not the sun go down upon your wrath". (Ephesians 4:26) God has forgiven you and me; should we not forgive one another?

Forgive and get right with God and your neighbour now. Do it today .

YOKES

How a yoke is made and shaped to fit the owner is important. If they are a bad fit they can be rough, unbalanced and hurtful. If they are well made, they will be a good fit and share the load equally across the shoulders. But however well they are made, the load must be balanced equally on both sides, sharing the burden.

Jesus the carpenter must have made many yokes in His time and 'yokes' with His trademark on them are easy and make our burdens light and easy to carry because He takes the weight off our shoulders. Read Matt. 11:28-30 and you'll see what I am talking about.

IN THE PITS

When we are 'in the pits' it is often because we need a service, or the Lord wants to speak to us or to make an adjustment to our lives. Obey the Course Marshal; He can see the smoke coming from your engine long before you will, or that one of your tyres is losing its tread or wants a bit more air!

THE LAST WILL AND TESTIMONY...

Jesus made a Will - to be the Saviour of the world. But a Will does not come into effect until the one who has made it has died. So Jesus did that too - for all of us, on the cross; so that all who believe in Him might be the beneficiaries of that Will, which, through His rising to life again, gives us eternal life. Thank you Jesus, for doing that for me.

APPEARANCES AND DISAPPEARANCES

When Jesus arose from the dead He spent much of the time between then and His Ascension appearing to and disappearing from His Disciples - some would say like a ghost. But ghosts do not do the things Jesus did - like talking to His friends, eating in front of them and with them, walking and just being with them in as real a presence as He had before His death - even gathering flotsam and making a fire on the sea shore to cook them breakfast. He disappeared and appeared before them, yes: but perhaps that was to prepare them for the day of His Ascension when He would leave them for a longer period to return to His Father in heaven. They witnessed His leaving; they had heard the promises that He had given them earlier - "I go to prepare a place far you". "I will return to receive you; to fetch you to be with Me for ever, where I am". The angels who appeared to the disciples on the mountain top reminded them of these promises. He would come again. Meanwhile they had work to do. To "go into all the world and preach the gospel to the whole of creation". It is the inescapable job of all who call themselves by His Name to help towards the completion of that task, so that when He comes again, we will hear Him plainly say - "Well done! Now let's go home together".

I'LL WALK BESIDE YOU

"But Peter followed Him at a distance" - Matt.26:55. Lord, I want to follow You closely, not at a distance. Help me to do that. That I may be under your protection, hear Your voice, not lose the way or in any way become separated from You. Because I need that close relationship with You.

The best guide is the one who is prepared to go with you all the way - not just give you directions and then leave you to work it out for yourself.

"Can you tell me the way to .... ?" Which of the following directions are the most helpful?

"Sorry, I don't know. I am a stranger around here".

"Yes: first left, second right, up the hill, fourth left, under the bridge, second right down the alley way and you're there". Or are you? I'm lost: and five minutes later, you are too!

"Yes, I am going that way, I'll walk along with you and show you and we'll get there together". You feel safe and secure.

A LIFT UP WITH NO LET DOWN

"For this reason I kneel before the Father ... I pray that He will, out of His glorious riches, strengthen you with power through His Spirit in your inner being" (Eph.3:14)

Like old watches, life has a tendency to run down. It needs rewinding. Prayer does just that; it rewinds the spring of life.

Instead of turning to prayer, many tinker with the hands and try to push them around - and finish up in breakdown or burn out. The speed of a model train is never relative to the real thing. Eventually the spring breaks or the transformer burns out.

Jesus often withdrew into the wilderness and prayed. (Luke 5:15-16) Prayer is a lift up with no let down. Jesus replenished His resources with prayer. All the more should we.

PSALM 46

> "God is our refuge and strength -
> <u>present help</u>. So we won't
> fear; even though
> the earth gives way,
> mountains fall,
> waters roar and foam,
> mountains quake,
> nations are in uproar
> kingdoms fall.
> <u>God is our fortress</u>.
> <u>Come see what He has done</u> –
> Wars cease,
> Bows are broken,
> Spears shattered,
> Shields burnt,
> Then - after all the noise and tumult, we get –
> "Be still and know that I am God",
> "I will be exalted."
> The Lord Almighty is with us;
> God is our refuge.

EASTER - A LONG WEEKEND

It's going home time on the Thursday evening before Easter. No more work until next Tuesday. Some of us will be packing to go away; some planning a spring-time blitz on the garden; others just a quiet, relaxing time with the family. The beginning of a long weekend.

Jesus took 'a long weekend' for us; a very long weekend. Hardly an Easter break. No holiday with hot cross buns and Easter eggs for Him! Yet both are there to remind us of what He did for us - for me. The mark on the bun reminds me of the cross - all that it meant for Him; all that it means for me. And the egg speaks to me of new life in Him - breaking out of the dark shell of the tomb to give us the promise of new life in a dark world. The whole episode is the link between His body and His blood - and everlasting life.

STEPPING STONES OR OPPORTUNITY

Do I allow circumstances to control my faith and my attitudes and my feelings? Or do I work towards making my faith so strong that feelings and attitudes and circumstances are subservient to it and become stepping stones rather than stumbling blocks to growth, and obstacles become opportunities because I put my faith in God and trust Him to make them so? "He turns our weaknesses into His opportunities so that the glory goes to Him". (2.Cor. 12:7-10)

OPERATION SLATE

On Saturday 29th December 2001 a service of Thanksgiving and Celebration was held for the life of Roger Lloyd Wood, the husband of Sarah, our Rector of Heanton with Marwood, in North Devon. As Hadyn's contribution to the service for his father he read us one of Roger's poems.

"In 1973, the Wood and Gilbert families moved to Cornwall. Mum and Dad bought a cottage near St Austell, which had a fire without a hearth. This is Dad's account of how we came by one."

> I tell the tale of the Gilwood clan,
> Two of woman and nine of man,
> Who one fine January afternoon,
> All descended upon Pentewan
> With coils of rope and webbing length
> We came to testify our strength,
> At the instigation of one named Quen –
> (If he'd been there we'd have been ten!);
> For he had seen down by the beach
> And not too difficult to reach,
> Some slabs of slate too good to leave
> And which we'd come down to retrieve.

P.T.O.

Operation Slate continued……..

A ruined building hid the loot,
Perhaps I should describe the route.
It really wasn't very far
To carry them up to the car.
Along a path, across a stream,
Through marsh and mire; picture the scene,
Under barbed wire, upon our knees
To a field with a slope of fifty degrees.
Pushing and pulling, heaving and straining
'Til muddy and exhausted we reached the railing.
Then at long last we arrived at the road;
Job done? No, back for the second load!

The other slab was even bigger,
Three hundredweight would be a fair figure;
And that's not light when you try to struggle
With your leg immersed in a muddy puddle;
Or pulling uphill with your back to the slope,
You can't look round, you can only hope
That a dear old cow or a dear little sheep
Hasn't left in your path a dirty great heap
Of you know what – for there's plenty around
On that steep, green slippery, muddy ground.
Onward and upward without any fuss
Until all is stored in the mini-bus.

So thank you lads and lasses all
For answering our urgent call:
For strength and vigour, muscle and sweat;
Without it the slate would have been there yet.
When it's cut and installed in our homely grate,
We'll invite you to tea with a great big plate
Of toasted tea-cakes and buns galore,
Which we'll enjoy as we sit on the floor,
And recall the day when the Gilwood band
Recovered the treasure of Pentewan Sand.

January 1977   Roger Wood